It's Israel's Birthday!

Ellen Dietrick

photographs by Tod Cohen

KAR-BEN
PUBLISHING

Yom Ha'atzmaut, Israel Independence Day, is celebrated annually on the 5th of the Hebrew month of Iyar, the anniversary of the establishment of the State of Israel (May 14, 1948). Families gather for public ceremonies and parades and often go on hikes and picnics.

For the children of CBI Preschool.
I am honored to be a part of your journey.
And to my grandparents, Carl and Rose Lifland,
who taught me a love of Israel. —E.D.

Text copyright © 2008 by Ellen Dietrick
Photos copyright © 2008 by Tod Cohen

Kar-Ben Publishing, Inc.
A division of Lerner Publishing Group
241 First Avenue North
Minneapolis, MN 55401 U.S.A.
1-800-4-KARBEN

Website address: www.karben.com

Library of Congress Cataloging-in-Publication Data

Dietrick, Ellen 1977–
    It's Israel's birthday / by Ellen Dietrick ; illustrated by Tod Cohen.
       p.   cm.
    ISBN-13: 978–0–8225–7668–6 (lib. bdg : alk. paper)
    1. Israel—Pictorial works—Juvenile literature. I. Cohen, Tod. II. Title.
DS107.5.D54 2008
394.262—dc22   2007011222

Manufactured in the United States of America
1 2 3 4 5 6 – JR – 08 07 06 05 04 03

It's Yom Ha'atzmaut, Israel's birthday.

Let's board a plane
and fly to Israel to celebrate.

We've landed at Ben Gurion Airport.
Josh is having his passport stamped.

The tour bus has stopped at a
kibbutz. They grow oranges here.

Mmm…sweet.

We're in Jerusalem and we're stopping at the shuk, the market. The fruits and vegetables make us hungry.

David is buying a kiddush cup as a
Bar Mitzvah gift for his big brother.

It's time for lunch. Here is a felafel stand.

Sophie likes salad in her felafel.
Emily likes French fries.

The Kotel is a wall that once surrounded the
Holy Temple. Many people come here to pray.

Benjy is tucking his prayer in the wall.

Much of Israel is hot, dry desert.

Archeologists dig here
to learn about ancient people.

Now it's time to cool off with a swim.

The Dead Sea has so much salt
you can float without trying.

In Israeli schools, the children learn
to read and write in Hebrew.

We're learning how to count in Hebrew.

We've come to the big city of Tel Aviv
for Israel's birthday parade.

Everyone is marching – farmers, soldiers, teachers, even the felafel man.

Time to board the plane and fly home.
Shalom, chaverim. Goodbye, new friends.

Happy Yom Ha'atzmaut!
Happy Birthday, Israel!

Israel's Birthday Hats

What you need:
Strips of colored paper,
    3 inches wide
Strips of colored paper,
    1 inch wide
White paper cut into rectangles
Blue paper cut into strips and
    triangles
Stickers
Scissors and glue
Stapler or tape

What you do:
1. To make the hat, staple or tape two 3-inch strips together to fit around your head like a crown. Add another strip across the top as shown.
2. To make zig zags, fold 1-inch strips like an accordion.
3. To make flags, paste the blue triangles and strips onto the white rectangles.
4. Decorate your hat with stickers, flags, and zigzags.

Wear your hat to march in Israel's birthday parade!